Also by Bob Smith
"Your Soul
an Owners' Manual"

POLITICAL CORRECTNESS

The Enemy Within

BOB SMITH

WESTBOW
PRESS®
A DIVISION OF THOMAS NELSON
& ZONDERVAN

WestBow Press books may be ordered through booksellers or by contacting:

WestBow Press
A Division of Thomas Nelson & Zondervan
1663 Liberty Drive
Bloomington, IN 47403
www.westbowpress.com
1 (866) 928-1240

ISBN: 978-1-9736-2123-2 (sc)
ISBN: 978-1-9736-2122-5 (e)

Library of Congress Control Number: 2018902413

Print information available on the last page.

WestBow Press rev. date: 03/15/2018

Contents

Introduction vii

Storm Warnings... 1
Battle Plan 3
   The Enemy 5
   The Weapons 8
Our Bill of Rights 12
Some PC Attacks on Our Liberty 13
The right to be born 14
Parents and the PC Problem 15
The Game Changer 17
Extremism 18
God and Our Rights 20
PC vs. Thanksgiving 22
Immigration and PC 24
Islamophobia 26
Sanctuary Cities 27
California vs. USA 29
The Gospel of 'no'... the PC mantra 32
George Washington's Church 34
Abuse of our freedoms 35
   The Attack Plan 39
All Out Assault on PC 40
Demographics 42
The Result 45

Addendum 47
About the Author 49

INTRODUCTION

It began as a gentle breeze… nothing more than a friendly "Happy Holiday", instead of "Merry Christmas" which might offend a non-Christian.

Soon, the soft breeze became a flurry of potential words which could be offensive. Racist, sexist, homophobic. Our vocabulary, we noticed, was being sharply censored by "well meaning' citizens who quietly saw themselves as political correction watchdogs.

In our busy, everyday lives, we went along with "Happy Holidays" but thought little of the cultural change that was inching along under our very nose.

That soft zephyr of a breeze has now become a full storm, hatching PC 'citizen police'. All around us is evidence of this challenge to the very core of Americanism. The media have become active partners in this assault. Our flag, our history, our religion, our speech, and yes, our way of life, all are under attack.

Storm Warnings...

WAKE UP AMERICA

There is a storm brewing in our midst. A very dangerous storm, but as all category five killer hurricanes, this is still only a stage two… bothersome, but its' potential death blows are not as yet apparent.

It began as a gentle breeze, the fresh air of polite consideration for one another. A simple idea.… "Happy Holiday" … greeting instead of the universal "Merry Christmas". We really don't know his/her religion, therefore, out of courtesy, "Happy Holiday" is safe.

Gradually, as happens with many good ideas, it was co-opted by academia… fertile ground for seed to take hold and grow into a weed. Suddenly, people in the professions became watchful, not to offend anyone. Sexist, racist, homophobic over- tones crept into our lexicon. This is serious stuff. The next step, of course, was the idea that if we were to be afraid to be offensive, we had a right, even a duty, to correct others when they were 'offensive'.

The weed has now matured into a 'cultural police' responsibility we all share.

Now, even more fertile ground has become infected with political correctness.

Politicians, always looking for a new way to put down an opponent, have descended from gentlemanly behavior, into attacks based upon the opponents' character.

So, we have seen considerate thoughts become weeds of discontent. Those weeds now have become a true cultural disease.

The disease has become cancerous and, as such, a very real danger. All Americans should, at this point realize the terrible potential for our way of life.

Under attack   *Our Flag*
          Our religion
          Our speech
          Our police
          Our morality

Special importance… Our children whose education now contains germs of evil such as gender self-identification, and the like, must be protected from this immorality.

Parents, we must get hold of this problem. Our school kids are targeted.*

**see addendum*

Our complacency invites attack.
WHAT ARE WE TO DO ABOUT IT?
Read on, my friend

BATTLE PLAN

The first, and most important requisite. is a deep and steadfast commitment to defeat the growing P.C. movement. Stop it while still in its infancy

Yes, it is still new enough that most Americans dislike parts of the whole but do not yet, grasp the serious challenge it represents to our freedoms, and in fact, our very form of government.

So how do we stop it? By a national uproar, a statement loud and clear to our leaders and courts that P.C. in all its venomous forms is not acceptable. We interrupt it with town hall meetings attended by overflow crowds protesting anti-American rules. Constant barrages of mail and nonstop phone calls to our elected officials will remind them of their constituents wishes and presence at the next ballot box meeting. These P.C. rules, were put in place not only by weak politicians, but also, to a large degree, by corporate leaders who cave in at the thought of a P.C. boycott. If our corporate leaders fear the 'political police', let them ponder a public boycott of their product. The NFL feels a steadily increasing loss of revenue, due to fan boycotts of TV games and refusal to attend games at which our flag is disrespected. Bravo!

Grass Roots

It all must start at the town level. Our mayors, town or city council members must be made aware that their re-election depends upon their response to the will of the people, ... a true example of democracy at work.

Always, the pressure must flow upwards, progressively from local to county, state pols and finally to those we elect in Washington. Using those communications the average citizen has at his disposal, pressure can be applied in direct proportion to the volume of written and phone activity.

Again, we know absolutely, that the way to a politicians' heart is though the vote count.

THE ENEMY

The Cabal

"The main obstacle to a stable and just
world order is the United States."
Soros...Wikipedia

The Merriam-Webster dictionary defines 'cabal' as "the contrived schemes of a group of persons secretly united in a plot to over- turn a government."

The radical use of the innocent sounding phrase 'political correctness' has been adopted by a shadow group, using PC as the opening round in the battle for control of the American government. An adherent of liberal/ progressive ideas, George Soros is a main contributor to the PC movement. His cabal chose to remain nameless, for obvious reasons. According to press statements, they are of the multi billionaire class.

Power is their game
absolute power.

The operational underlings of the cabal have shown themselves to be leaders of the democratic party in the U.S. congress. Nancy Pelosi in the house, and Chuck Schumer in the senate, keep their troops on a tight leash

Check out some of the important voting patterns. Remember the Obama Care "wheel and deal? The congress, and the public had no idea of the 'back room', midnight decisions about the bill. When asked, Pelosi replied "You will know after you pass the bill and read it". The final product, some two thousand pages, was passed with 219 democratic votes. This use of raw power by Pelosi was an early test. Why would a congress person vote, as they did, on an unseen controversial bill?

Madison once said "Power corrupts, absolute power absolutely corrupts".

Know your enemy

THE WEAPONS

Social Media

Twitter, Facebook, Google, Instagram, etc. offer the potential to organize a powerful movement to combat the 'political correctness' craze that is sweeping the country. It will take a knowledgeable, public spirited person. group or club, to put together a strong program and deliver it to millions who are already networking and tweeting about a host of personal issues.

We saw how they organized by the millions for Trump during his campaign. This will be a campaign to save America. It would be well if there could be established branches of these media, directed at kids from grades K to 12. They are our most important demographic... most vulnerable, most likely to be already targeted for PC indoctrination. Also, most likely, they will enter adulthood and assume positions of leadership, to teach the 'gospel of PC' to their own children, and subsequently to future generations.

PC is invading almost every aspect of American life. As the cover of this book points out, our flag, religion, freedom of speech, police, morality, education, and even the right to become a newborn, are in jeopardy. A full blown, dynamic response, by an angry, voting, citizenry is our best, and I'm afraid, our only hope to defeat this scourge upon our sensibilities and our country.

Are you the one to start the ball rolling?

We remember those glorious words of President Lincoln... "Government of the people, by the people and for the people".

Our founding fathers gave us 'Power to the People' in the form of a bicameral congress. This body can change the law to meet the will of the people, even to the degree of amending the constitution, if necessary.

Just to regroup here for a moment, I opened with the title "Battle Plan". And believe me, we are in a battle, *a battle of ideas*. Every American is surely aware of our revolution against the king. It began with an idea. Freedom in the form of government by the people and for the people, rather than by a king and for a king, was the idea... a grass roots idea.

A couple of well known, successful revolutions, orchestrated from the grass roots level, come to mind.... The Russian people, upset with the Tsar, fought and won, although they lost control and faced a new loss of freedom by a new government.

The French people launched a successful, albeit bloody overthrow of the king, and founded a Republic based upon the idea of freedom.

Of the three IDEA based revolutions described above, ours is the only one still in its original form although it had to be defended in a civil war.

Our present *battle of ideas* is a peaceful confrontation with evil ideas, designed to rob us of our rights, using the guise of "never offending anyone" by our speech, religion or otherwise.

The <u>Declaration</u> of <u>Independence</u> (excerpt)

'We hold these truths to be self-evident, that all Men are created equal, that they are endowed by their Creator with certain unalienable Rights, that among these are Life, Liberty and the pursuit of Happiness. – That to secure these rights, Governments are instituted among Men, deriving their just powers from the consent of the governed'.

Following this announcement of separation from the British Empire, America sealed the deal with a victory and expelled the red coats from our shores.

At Philadelphia, our founders crafted a constitution and ten amendments known as the Bill of Rights which the states ratified in 1789.

Our return to true freedom and morality will be a peaceful affair. It will be a people driven return to the ideals written by Jefferson, Adams, Madison and those whose dream was a free people pursuing happiness.

It will require a massive voice of 'the people', so strong that our elected will decide to enforce the law in the cases relating to the first amendment, apply by law the right to be born, encourage police to enforce the law, and litigate against evil regulations concerning our children.

This is as it should be. Government from the bottom up, not by the Hollywood crowd and other elite controlling congress.

We <u>CAN do it.</u>

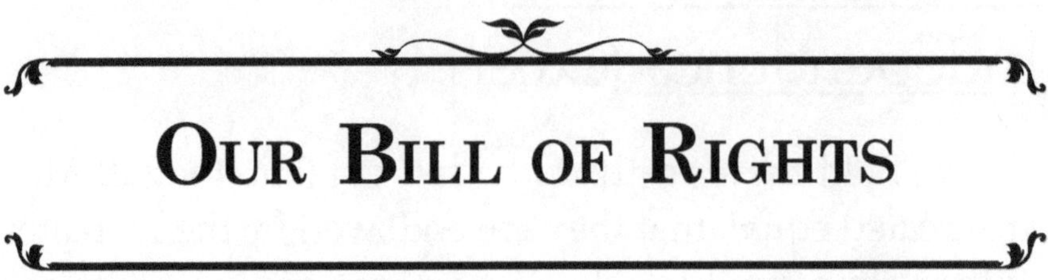

OUR BILL OF RIGHTS

These ten amendments were added to the constitution in order to spell out, for all time, those God given, unalienable Rights promised in the Declaration of Independence.

Amendment 1... Freedom of religion, speech, the press, rights of assembly and petition.
Amendment 2... Right to bear arms
Amendment 3... Housing of soldiers
Amendment 4... Search and arrest warrants
Amendment 5... Rights in criminal cases
Amendment 6... Rights to a fair trial
Amendment 7... Rights in civil cases
Amendment 8... Bails, fines and punishment
Amendment 9... Rights retained by the people
Amendment 10.. Rights retained by the states and the people

America has grown and thrived for two hundred twenty eight years because of these protections and our constitutional government. The Bill is, with the constitution, the finest document of its kind ever produced. The PC gang is hard at work trying to rob us of these rights.

Some PC Attacks on Our Liberty

THE RIGHT TO BE BORN

In an astounding decision, the Supreme Court overturned one third of Jefferson's God given right to "Life, Liberty and the Pursuit of Happiness". Life includes of course, the right not to be killed before birth.

Abortion mills have become, since the 1973 Roe v. Wade decision, a real growth industry. (no pun intended). Sadly, in 1976 alone we lost 988,267* potential citizens. Since 1973 America has suffered 60,071,345* abortions. By comparison, the Nazis will forever be hated for killing an estimated 6,000,000 Jews. The slaughter of babies continues in the U.S.A.

***Source: Guttmacher Center for Population Research and CDC, Atlanta**

Today, it is considered politically incorrect to question a woman's right to choose. However, it is politically <u>correct</u> to choose death.

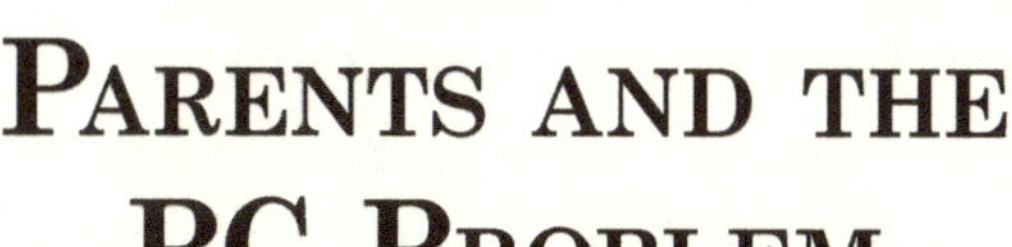

Parents and the PC Problem

Step one for caring parents is to prepare for educating sons and daughters to be become aware and familiar with the dangers built-in to the culture of 'political correctness' It's never too early to begin. Some schools are already training kids to choose whether to be known as boys or girls, and, even which race they choose to be. They even offer 'gender free' bathrooms. All this from grades K to 12.

This indoctrination is designed to prepare the next generation of leaders to govern with political correctness. Scary, isn't it?

Beyond training, it is now more than ever, important to check on the school or college selected. Do they allow the pledge of allegiance to our flag? Do they permit prayers in class? Also, very important, do they teach American history and our constitution?

A decent college degree today can cost more than $100,000. Be sure of what you are buying!

The PC poison has infected colleges and universities across the land. The need by the radical left now, is to control free speech. This need to control, goes far beyond 'offensive speech'. It has long been a practice of schools of higher education, to invite guest speakers, highly valued for their expertise in a given field of study, to address the student body. This source of guest information is of unique value, coming from out- side academia by an expert.

Any guest speaker who is not PC oriented is now usually greeted by a loud band of protesters using the usual tools of hate… bullhorns to shout and hateful signs carried by rowdy students, sometimes wearing masks. The speaker who bravely proceeds to the auditorium is drowned out by booing, cat calls and general wild noise. He/she then departs.

The students are now further
empowered by their ignorance.

To reject a gifted speaker, due to his or her political leanings, is to reject the very idea of liberal education. An open mind, anxious to investigate both sides of an issue before making a decision, is the very reason for higher learning.

It is sad and so ironic that so many of todays' students rely upon PC in their decision making process. School officials often excuse this behavior either because they themselves are teachers of PC, or because they are fearful of parental reaction and subsequent loss of endowments. It's a case of inmates running the asylum.

THE GAME CHANGER

At this point, the parents, who pay the bills, have the best opportunity to pressure the school board to return to a traditional curriculum.

Again, organization is the key. A large meeting of parents, attended by an invited board member of the school, will get the attention of the administrators.

Invite he press. The promise is a major parental rally on campus to protest the new curricula of leftist, PC oriented study. Parents are demanding a return to a code of civil conduct, a focused, traditional curriculum, as well as citizenship training,

When significant numbers of parents threaten to withdraw students, because of the PC abomination, those parents will be heard, loud and clear. They are now talking 'pocketbook' language. Take away the exaggerated tuitions and, of course, the usual endowments and watch the return to a value oriented education!

Organize and you will win.
Remember, "Money talks, nobody walks",

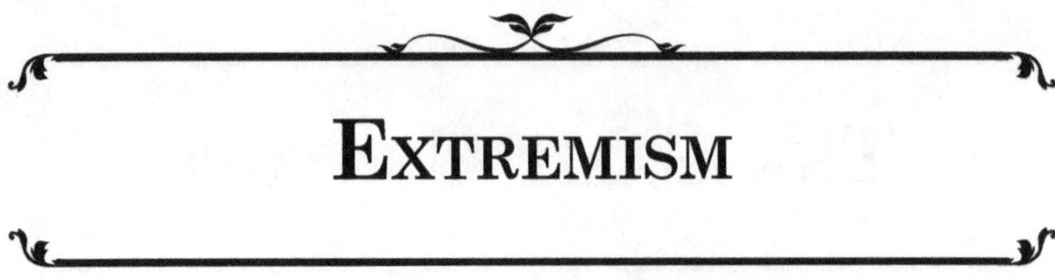

EXTREMISM

Extremism is often a projection of falsely assumed authority by the speaker, on the right, as well as the left.

"My way or the highway"

This purposeful stoppage of debate has a dual affect. It announces the supposed superiority of the speaker. It elevates the angst of the other party in the discussion

We now have no chance of negotiation for a mutually agreeable result of the issue

Extremism is the very nature of "Political Correctness". Advocates of this policy falsely claim to be authoritative judges of acceptable and non- acceptable human behavior. As such, it is their intent to dictate to us, as less knowledgeable folks, the "correct" attitude. However, the outcome in some cases can be as we shall soon see, violent behavior ..

God Bless You!

Examples of everyday words
and phrases considered
to be objectionable by the
'politically correct police'…

Merry Christmas
Happy Easter
Happy Thanksgiving
Thank God!
God bless you
For heaven's sake
Godspeed

Now really! These are truly no more than expressions of neighborly love. Is there actually some damage done to the human psyche by these words, or is this just another pitiful example of extremism by the PC 'police?'

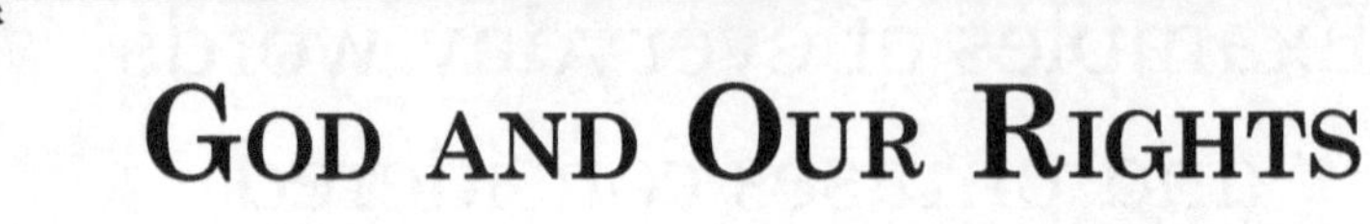

GOD AND OUR RIGHTS

God is alive and well in America. We, of many different faiths, are all one people, loving one God. We are devout citizens, serious about our Creator, or, serious non- believers.

Our forefathers, many of whom were descendants of refugees fleeing Europe and religious persecution, were very much aware of the dangers of religious intolerance.

When crafting the Bill of Rights, they were very specific about religion.

"Congress shall make no law respecting an establishment of religion, or prohibiting the free exercise thereof."

Today's brand of 'political correctness' is totally intolerant of any type of religious discourse, because 'someone might be offended'. They are peppering our courts and institutions with lawsuits objecting to everything from prayer in school to public display of crosses. This attempt to control our expression of faith must not stand.

Our Right of Assembly, is guaranteed by the first Amendment of the Constitution.

Here we have too many examples of gross abuse to enumerate. A ground swell of protest marches, ending in riots, property damage, and even death, as if that was not enough, have given birth to a new and powerful, divisive PC battle cry… "Black lives matter".

A police officer was tried and acquitted of murder by a jury in 2013 in Ferguson, Missouri. The ensuing riots drew protesters from eighteen different cities, shouting "black lives matter". BLM groups have metastasized to a network of more than 40 chapters as of this writing

Well organized black power has cowed mayors around the country into ceasing 'stop and search' and other previously effective crime control measures.

"Black lives <u>ALSO</u> matter" would have been an entirely understandable, sympathetic message garnering support for the cause. As it was, BLM contributed greatly to the racial divide in America. The rioting which grew out if the Ferguson demonstration was an abuse of the first amendment right of assembly.

PC vs. Thanksgiving

No American is exempt from the ire of the PC gang.

History teaches us that the pilgrims were celebrating the harvest, as well as life in the new world by the grace of God. The Indians co-celebrated the harvest.

It turns out that our latest generation of PC philosophers have discovered the "truth". The combined joy of this feast was short lived. Boatloads of refugees from British persecution of those citizens who rejected the reformation of Henry VIII, were landing in the new world. From Plymouth to Jamestown they came, occupying Indian space. Soon enough, land battles raged, lasting almost four hundred years until the white man captured the land from sea to sea. This action is known in some circles as "manifest destiny".

That story not withstanding' The first thanksgiving celebration was a joyous moment in time which should be remembered and celebrated as such.

The PC police are offering the following alternatives for Thanksgiving Day...

"A commemoration of genocide and American Imperialism"

or

"An acknowledgement of the genocide of indigenous people that is central to the creation of the United States".

The PC intellectual crime is to rob us of our history. Many of us may remember the shocking news videos of Taliban destruction by dynamite, of ancient, beautiful temples and relics… a shameful act of eliminating history. The same purposeful loss of the library at Alexandria was by the Romans et al, who burned at least 40,000 scrolls.

By their action of attempting to rob history, the PC movement joins the Taliban in the spirit of destroying our past.

IMMIGRATION AND PC

Every country in the world has borders. It is said that if you don't have a border, you don't really have a country. It is obvious that without an established border with check points, people, goods and illegal substances could freely pass back and forth between countries.

We, the people of America, have a serious problem with our southern border. An estimated 6-7 million immigrants have entered the U.S. illegally*. Each year over 500,000 people enter our country illegally*.

The prime avenue of entry for narcotics is through the Mexican border. In truth, that avenue has become a highway. Terrorists have no problem entering our land via this highway.

President Trump has promised to build a wall on that border. Recent history proves that walls work. The Berlin wall, a twelve foot high concrete barrier topped with barbed wire extended for ninety six miles and very effectively stopped passage in either direction. A good idea for America to protect our southern border, right? Not according to the PC crowd. Claiming it is discrimination against Hispanics, they have lobbied very effectively against the wall.

This is another example of political correctness run amok. By fanning the flames of racism, they are doing an enormous dis-service to our country. Not only is their position a racist slur, but it is a major factor in the attempt to win by dividing, instead of uniting Americans.

Can we, as citizens, calmly watch this travesty nightly on the evening news and then just move on to the next issue?

Are we ready to do something about it?

Well, read on my friends

An answer may be in your future

*** Source: U.S. Department of Homeland Security**

ISLAMOPHOBIA

This is about infiltrators, "no go" enclaves, Muslim terrorists and just plain Muslims. Of course, it's mainly about being politically correct. If that's the way it will be, this is about Muslims, period. We wouldn't want to offend!

Islamic terrorists, infiltrators, and the horrors of Sharia law are words that might offend some.

Of course, it is true that Muslims who are terrorists and who practice Sharia law in "no go" enclaves here and abroad, are murderers and people who perform circumcision and other horrors on pre-teen girls <u>are</u> monsters.

ENOUGH! The words are offensive, but the deeds are truly unimaginable.

'No go' zones are Islamic enclaves too dangerous for first responders to enter. France, Belgium, even Sweden and our USA have such places*. These immigrants have no desire to assimilate or accept our culture. Surprise … Dearborn Michigan, known as the "Baghdad of America" has the largest mosque in North America. *(I'll be happy to send a list of 'no go' Enclaves in America – see authors note on back cover for details)*

SANCTUARY CITIES

The most outrageous and physically dangerous idea ever designed by civil government in America, is called 'sanctuary cities'. This bonehead plan, devised by mayors, is meant to protect illegal immigrants from seizure and deportation by federal authorities. This safe- haven status applies even to illegals when released from jail for most crimes committed after entry into the US. The police are not even permitted to stop and question them.

The very act of crossing our border illegally is a crime. After conviction of a second crime they are still, in most cases, under protection from deportation by local authorities. This insane policy is now being advocated for counties as well as cities. Most incredible is that six of our fifty states have announced themselves to be sanctuary states

Why, you may ask, would a mayor put the well being of a felon ahead of the best interest and safety of his citizens? In truth, there is only one answer to that, although they will never admit it. As elected officials, they invariably feel that their first job is to get re-elected.

Therefore, votes, in this case Hispanic votes, are the prime consideration. But, you say, they were elected to serve the entire population. Correct. So join the effort to eliminate political correctness from our national scene. Help America to return to the original values as described by Jefferson and company.

As we implied in the beginning of this book, as Americans, we are losing our way. The fact that we can stand for this most stupid and egregious policy should be a wake- up call.

The animals are taking over the farm!

California vs. USA

The state of California, has become a sanctuary state in response to the 'politically correct' or PC dogma. Governor Brown chose popularity with the Hispanic community over the rule of law and the safety of our country as a whole. To mask the fact that illegal border crossing is a crime, Brown re-names the illegals 'undocumented residents'.

The ugly story begins at the Mexican border. This is the gateway for fentanyl, a drug called "manufactured death" by the Drug Enforcement Administration (DEA). The journey for fentanyl begins as the chemical ingredients are shipped from China to Mexico. The mix is processed, packaged and smuggled across the border into America. Tunnels are the main method, as we have seen on Fox TV… rooms full of the captured stuff on display by the DEA. It is no secret that the Mexican cartels are mainly responsible for this trade. It is also true that vast amounts of fentanyl end their journey in New England.

The result is a plague causing the highest rate of fentanyl related deaths in America.

"It's like no other epidemic I've ever seen" said Mike Ferguson*, special agent in charge of the New England

DEA office. He told the Boston Globe that it's sweeping Maine, New Hampshire and Vermont as well.

Accessory to the fact

Governor Brown welcomes illegals. protects them, even grants them drivers licenses* which they can only use as identification if they don't have auto insurance. The license does give them false ID.

*806,000 undocumented residents (illegals) have received driver licenses.

*DMV.

His choice of politically correct popularity contributes heavily to the drug problem around the country and especially in New England.

One question in all this
Are we, as a nation losing it?

California is fighting border control, treating criminal illegals as family because of political correctness, while death drugs pour across the border from Mexico to New England.

"But the drugs are only passing through the border". Oh, I see.

What's wrong with you PC people?
Yes, we are losing it
thanks to PC.

What about this... "one people", from California to Maine, united under God and our constitution?

It's worth the fight!

It's worthy to note that those folks, who never want to offend anyone, are quite willing to fight for their version of open borders… even though they know that the path from China to Maine requires a complicit California border to pass the offensive, death dealing drugs on their way to 'offend' the citizens of New England.

THE GOSPEL OF 'NO'...
THE PC MANTRA

No, we must not pray openly in or around school or on the field of sport.

No, we cannot end state sponsored, paid abortions.

No, we should not use the term "radical Islamic terrorist".

No, we cannot halt the use of 'gender free' bathrooms in public schools.

No, we cannot object to 'self- identification' which permits students to choose which race they are, as well as which gender they are. Some schools will now adjust the records accordingly and maintain the students' privacy, even from his/her parents.

No, we cannot stop constant anti-police speech and demonstrations. Although the first amendment protects these activities, they are scandalous abuses of our freedom. Our first responders deserve thanks for all they do.

No, we must never offend anyone.

No, we must never say "Merry Christmas" or "Happy Hanukkah".

And 'No' so many more, so many, many…

No, we cannot stop the disrespect of our flag.

This anti-patriotism aspect of the PC movement does have a sinister side. Once we accept disrespect of Old Glory, we will be on a downward slope as far as respecting our country.

Know your enemy. The PC dogma of 'no' is merely the first step in the steady weening away of our traditional values. It will be a gradual process. Already, several U.S. congressmen have submitted legislation to repeal the first and second amendments of our constitution.

Can we stand by while PC philosophy is being developed in today's youth? Will they become the PC leaders of the next generation?

If, in our neglect of the dangers of PC, we fail to educate our sons and daughters about PC, the possibility of our republic one day becoming an oligarchy of elites ruling our nation is very real.

Reject PC. The conspiracy is very real.

It is 'The Enemy within".

GEORGE WASHINGTON'S CHURCH

The latest 'politically correct' atrocity is the removal of the plaque from Washington's place in the church he regularly attended. The reason was that someone might be offended by this religious designation.

This outrage is part of a designed campaign to break down and censor our American history and values. The pity of it is that it is not recognized as an assault upon our way of life, because it is being carried out incrementally, bit by bit.

The idea of never doing anything that might offend someone is a subterfuge for the real PC intent.

By altering, censoring or erasing our history, the new doctrine of PC, can more easily be taught to future generations, as though PC was really our past.

One by one, the attack continues. Our religion, our flag, our history are all targets in the conspiracy to dominate our country. Take warning. They are succeeding, bit by bit.

They are 'The enemy Within'.

Abuse of our Freedoms

Almost unrecognized, a cancer on our way of life has been spreading at an alarming rate.

POLITICAL CORRECTNESS or PC

This seemingly benign name is a cover for a concept, also innocent sounding, which is designed to gag free speech under the mantra "say or do nothing which may offend someone".

This supposed restriction would limit free speech about almost any subject, but especially those topics covered in the first amendment.

We will cover those topics, but first some egregious examples….

1. Delaware schools now allow students from grade K to 12, to 'self- identify'. That is to choose their gender and their race. This information is not given to parents. The lesson for kids is that it's OK to keep secrets from mom and dad.

2. Imagine that! It's now OK for a kid to decide if he/ she wants to be a boy or a girl, as well as to choose

which race he/she wants to be. This fits perfectly with the 'neuter gender' bathroom idea.

3. Colin Kaepernick, is now famous/infamous for starting a trend among some players on each NFL team to disrespect the American flag by not standing (kneeling) during the playing of our national anthem. As this type of protest spread like wildfire among some players on NFL teams, league management caved in by allowing this disrespect for Old Glory.

   The cover of a popular magazine featured a photo of Kaepernick with the award 'American hero of the year'. What about our military battling ISIS? Our cops on the front line against crime? PC evidently does not include these REAL heroes in the protection against offensive words.

   Flag burning, which the Supreme Court protects as a type of speech, is therefore legal, if not, at the very least, reprehensible.

* Many crosses have been removed from public view because they might offend someone.

* There have even been cases of crosses being removed from grave sites.

* It is a growing trend to forbid team prayers in public, among school/college football teams.

Many, if not most, public schools will not permit open prayers in class.

*Congress shall make no law respecting an
establishment of religion, or prohibiting
the free exercise thereof …
1ˢᵗ amendment excerpt)*

- PC enthusiasts claimed it was deplorable to offer prayers at the scene of the First Baptist church massacre.

What's a Person of Faith to do?

It's a sign of the times, I suppose, that lawyers are more successful in their anti-God program, than our ministers and priests seem to be in defending the faith.

The assault is on and we are the target.

The answer to political correctness....

- We will not surrender to the oppressors.
- We will be defenders of God's truth and man's God given rights.

To reject the censorship of the PC 'police' in favor of freedom is noble work.

"Let no one intimidate you to your own downfall. Refrain not from speaking at the proper time and hide not away your wisdom; for it is through speech that wisdom becomes known.

Even to the death fight for truth, and the

Lord your God will battle for you".

From the old testament – Sirach 5: 22-24, 28

A direct quote from the bible – The second letter of Paul to Timothy (excerpt)

Proclaim the word: be persistent whether it is convenient or inconvenient; convince, reprimand, encourage through all patience and teaching. For the time will come when people will not tolerate sound doctrine but, following their own desires and insatiable curiosity will accumulate teachers and will stop listening to the truth and will be diverted to myths. But you, be self- possessed in all circumstances; put up with hardship; perform the work of an evangelist; fulfill your ministry. ***2Timothy2:2-5***

Authors note: for you of faith, as well as all loyal citizens, this message from long ago is still valid today. We must stand firm against the forces of PC.

Proclaim the word. Contact your local politicians. Say no to political correctness.

Guidelines for Christians who must survive while standing firm against the PC 'gospel of no' atmosphere...

"Beware of false prophets, who come to you in sheep's clothing, but underneath are ravenous wolves. By their fruits you will know them."

Matthew 7:15,16

"There were also false prophets among the people, just as there will be false teachers among you, who will introduce destructive heresies... In their greed they will exploit you with fabrications."

2Peter2:1,3

Standing firm is easy when not seriously challenged. When your world, your friends and neighbors attack you for rejecting the ways of political correctness, it will hurt, but the rewards of righteousness will be yours. Stand firm against the evil teachers.

The Attack Plan

ALL OUT ASSAULT ON PC

Use it all, America, in a coordinated attack upon the forces of PC, who are trying to corrupt our children, our flag, our heritage, our rights…

All with an eventual goal of ruling America for the benefit of the shadow elite.

Your weapons are…

- Social media…
- Flood your local, state and national politicians with tweets and other internet media. Best if it can be an obvious coordinated effort, so it will be clear that the country is together on this. Thousands of thousands of votes at stake here, Mr./Ms. politician.
- Letter writing campaign. Pile up the mail on their desks… baskets full, preferably at the same time, each representing a vote.
- Phone calls are also valuable
- Town hall meetings are doubly effective if properly handled. Announce, well in advance, plans for a public, issue based meeting on a given date and time.

Coordinate with the local party for funding. Contact the potential opponent of your enemy in the next election. He will jump at the opportunity to speak at a town hall meeting. He will also be of help in advertising, as well as boosting attendance.

Most of all, get the word out door to door, grass root style. Also, very important, is the press. They will be happy to give a town hall meeting prime space in their daily editions. We do not want a poorly attended affair.

On the other hand, we saw the effect of over flowing crowds, standing in line to get in. What that did for President Trump was winning politics.

It's now our turn.

DEMOGRAPHICS

There are 35,000 recognized cities and towns in America. The medium to large cities will each will have a mayor and, at least one top ranked official. Let's figure conservatively 40% Republican and 40% Democrat, and 20%independent and only one official per city/ town. A hugely successful grass roots campaign might well generate 12,000 calls/ letters to congress <u>from mayors.</u>

<u>435 members of the House</u>
<u>100 senators</u>

That same hugely successful grass roots campaign should generate millions of letters/calls from fired up citizens. Factor in tweets and other social media contacts and you have unimaginable numbers.

That's a lot of voter pressure, folks!

Very rough estimates

Now, I know folks that you will probably disagree with my estimated 12,000 mayoral calls and letters. So do I. It is based upon no source except my visceral hope.

However, whether it will be 8,000 or 14,000 mayoral calls and letters, that's a lot of pressure from regular citizens who vote. It goes right to the heart of the politicians who are hoping to be re-elected.

It will happen, when and if when we Americans unite in a grass roots, nationwide movement to overcome those who would destroy our traditional American values. Those mayors who declare sanctuary cities, to curry favor with minority voters, while disregarding the safety of the majority of their citizens, must feel their wrath. It's a worthwhile effort to save the country we know and love, from the rule of a gang of elites.

For the past two hundred years, we have sent our youth to defend America. They have been our front line against aggression. They have given so much to save our Republic.

Now, once again, America is under attack. This time the fight is against an ideology. A pernicious idea which is barely recognizable, due to its nonconfrontational name...

'Political Correctness'.

We are in for the battle of our nations' very life. The battle now is one of ideas. At stake is our way of life, our freedom and our Republic.

This time America needs us, all of us, young and old. Our weapons are votes. The ballot box will determine winner and loser.

To win, we must recognize our enemy, get angry, unite and organize to deliver a protest so massive that our politicians, from local mayors to US senators and members of the house of representatives, will see the light.

In this case, the light is their reelection. They have the power to knock out PC… it comes from us.

"Power to the people".

THE RESULT

ADDENDUM

Raising children… then and now.

Born in 1931, meant growing up by learning life lessons. Mom, Dad and the kids all live together, eat at the same table and share the chores, and work each to his own ability.

Early on, I got a bike, a huge present in those years. As I learned to zip around the neighborhood, I was also taught that I could earn money by delivering newspapers door-door. Not yet ten, I would pick up the bundle the truck dropped off, and load my basket between the handle bars. Using a list, I would bring each paper to a front door, ring the bell, and continue. Each payday, I gave the money to mom who would return a small amount for ice cream and a movie. Each member of the house contributed. We said our nightly prayers and attended mass every Sunday. We were a close family.

My brother, nine years older, learned the same life lessons. He mowed lawns, shoveled snow, washed windows, plus kept the furnace going. He was in charge of the coal bins in the cellar. It was his responsibility to 'bank' the fire at night with enough coal to last till morning, at which time he would shovel out the ashes.

We had a good routine, Walt and I, until

Pearl Harbor, 1941. I was ten, and Walt went to war. Now, the coal, furnace, ashes were all mine. I also inherited his lawn, snow and window businesses. Time to grow up, Bob. After graduating high school, I took another lesson in growing up. Found out a lot more about the subject in five years working for Uncle Sam. In Korea, I think I learned some of what Walt learned in Europe.

Kids today – well what can I say?

They too, must learn life lessons. The subjects are different, but the attitude must be learned responsibility, obedience, love and family closeness

Parents today - well, what can I say?

If they did not learn those life lessons while growing up, It's not too late. Think about it. As young as toddler ages, the son or daughter learns love by example. He/she learns "no" in a gentle, repetitive manner. Learns by watching mom and dad, enjoys life, learns to live in harmony at home, and by extension in the community.

The child experiences the wonder of learning. Going places, seeing things. Mom, dad have a strong teaching role there. I don't think it's too complicated. It all springs from love. Sometimes tough love, but always love... love and trust.

Get all that together and life is good.

ABOUT THE AUTHOR

After serving five military years, I worked in the printing trades, eventually becoming a vice president of the union. When an opportunity came to become an entrepreneur, I opened a graphic arts/photography studio in New York.

American history has been a lifelong avocation. Emphasis on the political scene from Jefferson and crew to today's heated policy arguments... that is, from Alexander Hamilton to President Trump.

A strong belief in the adage "The Past is Prolog", has been of enough concern to cause me to write this warning to our countrymen about the growing danger of 'Political Correctness'. The book was a labor of love. Love of country, love of family, love of life. Life is good. Thank you for your interest.

Note; for those interested in 'No Go' cities I will gladly provide a list of European and American enclaves. Contact Bob Smith at my publisher See title page for details.